ROCKS AND MINERALS

© Aladdin Books 1988

Designed and produced by
Aladdin Books Ltd
70 Old Compton Street
London W1

*First published in the
United States in 1989 by*
Gloucester Press
387 Park Avenue South
New York, NY 10016

ISBN 0 531 17137 X

Library of Congress Catalog
Card Number: 88-83107

All rights reserved

Printed in Belgium

Author	Kathryn Whyman
	Science teacher & author of many children's books
Design	David West
	Children's Book Design
Editor	Scott Steedman
Researcher	Cecilia Weston-Baker
Illustrator	Louise Nevitt
Consultant	Ian Mercer
	Geology Museum, London

CONTENTS

Riches of the Earth	4
Rock and mineral formation	6
Metals from the Earth	8
Fuels from the Earth	10
Nuclear fuel	12
Ceramics	14
Bricks and tiles	16
Cement and stone	18
The silicon chip	20
Fertilizers and drugs	22
Gemstones	24
The story of a silicon chip	26
Fact File 1	28
Fact File 2	30
Index and glossary	32

Photographic Credits
Cover and page 10: Hutchison Library; intro pages and pages 5 and 21: Bruce Coleman; pages 4-5, 9, 12, 13 and 21 (inset): Photosource; pages 11, 14, 17 and 19: Zefa; page 18: NASA; pages 23, 24 and 25: Science Photo Library.

RESOURCES TODAY

ROCKS AND MINERALS

Kathryn Whyman

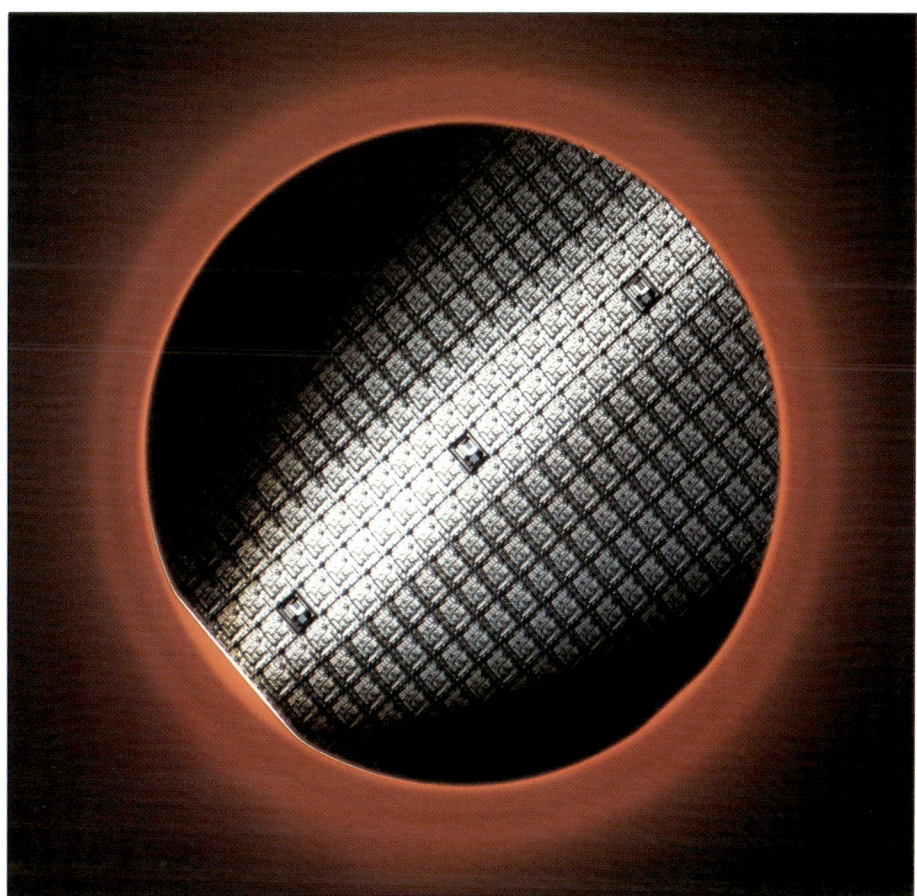

GLOUCESTER PRESS
New York · London · Toronto · Sydney

RICHES OF THE EARTH

The Earth is a rich resource. Rocks and minerals, the raw materials of the Earth, play an important part in our lives. Buildings, fertilizers, drugs and fuels are all made from rocks and minerals. Rocks and minerals are our oldest resource – stone age people were making and using stone axes two million years ago. But new uses are still being found for rocks and minerals. Today's computers would not work without silicon chips made from the mineral silicon dioxide.

A limestone cave in the United States

So what are rocks and minerals? Rocks are the solid materials of the Earth. Limestone and granite are common rocks. Like all rocks, they are made of chemical substances called minerals.

Minerals are the building blocks from which all rocks are made. Some rock types contain just one mineral. Limestone is the mineral calcite. But most rocks contain two or more different minerals. Granite is a mixture of two minerals – quartz and feldspar.

The inset shows lime being used to improve the soil

ROCK AND MINERAL FORMATION

The Earth is made up of over 3,000 minerals. Some of these minerals are rare. Others are plentiful, forming a great variety of rock types. Many of these rocks and minerals are mined because they are useful. Some are easy to mine. Rocks like granite may be found in large deposits by the surface. Halite (salt), a mineral, can be produced by evaporating sea water.

Igneous rocks
These rocks are formed when molten rock (magma) cools and becomes solid. Granite is created in the Earth's crust in this way (1). Sometimes magma bursts through the crust as lava and cools to form volcanic rocks like basalt (2).

Sedimentary rocks
Wind and water carry and deposit rock particles. Rivers lay down rocks like shale (3), and others like sandstone are deposited by the wind (4). Limestone is created when plant and animal skeletons build up on the beds of lakes and seas (5).

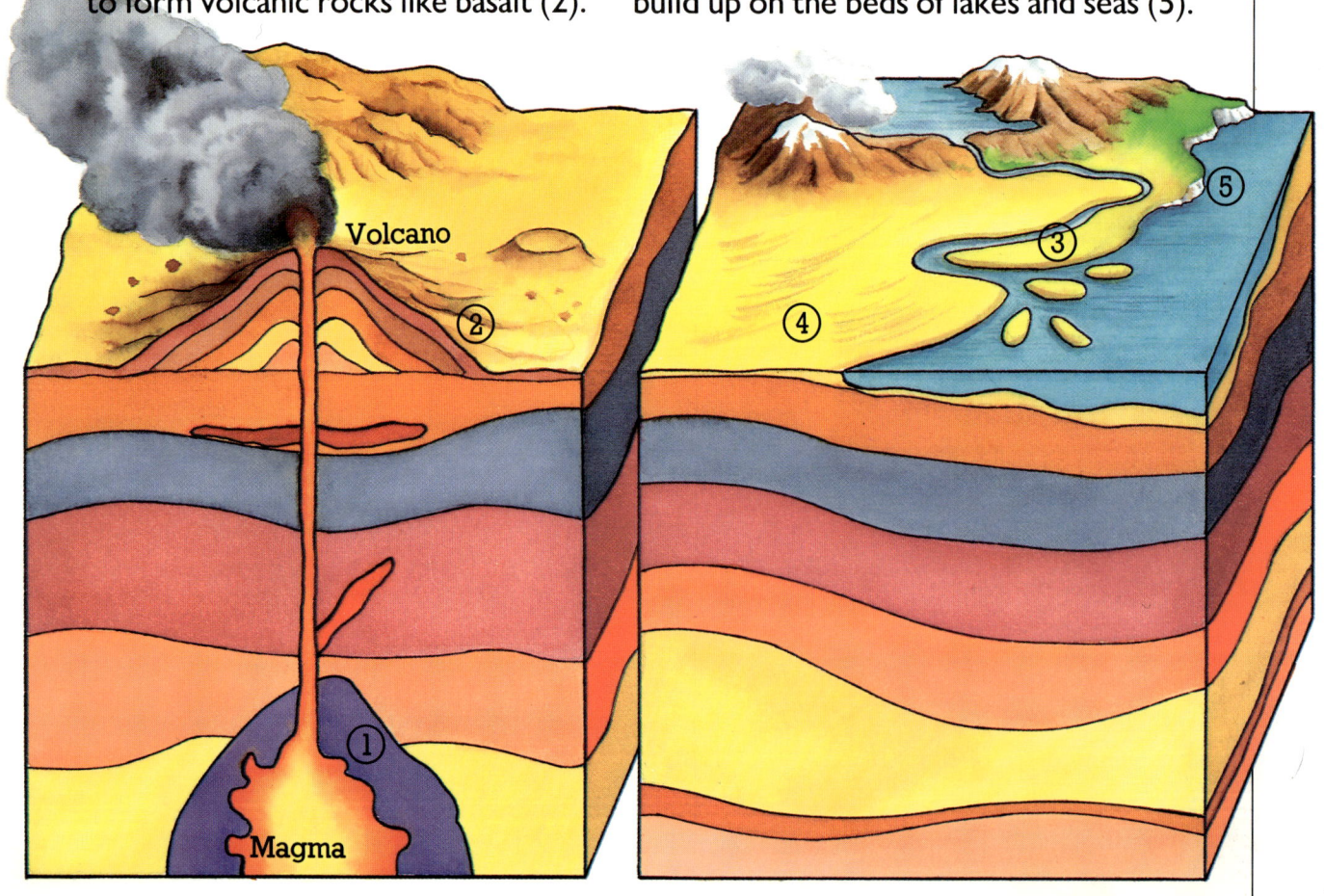

Other rocks and minerals are much harder to find. Many are only found deep beneath the Earth's surface. Diamonds are often found far underground. Most deposits of oil and gas are also deep below the surface – and some are covered by ocean water or polar ice. It is usually only worth mining rocks and minerals like these when they are found in large quantities in one place. Many tests and surveys are carried out before the exact location for a mine is chosen.

Metamorphic rocks
Rocks that are buried deep down may be changed into metamorphic rocks like slate by the pressure and heat (6). Magma may also heat the crust next to it so much that new rocks like marble are created (7).

Mineral deposits
Many valuable minerals are deposited by water. Some, like iron minerals, come from water left over when magma cools (8). Others, such as copper minerals, are formed by trapped sea water which is warmed up (9).

METALS FROM THE EARTH

Metals are an important group of mineral products. They are used in so many ways that it is hard to imagine life without them. Iron is used to make steel for building, copper makes electric wires, and aluminum is used to make all kinds of things from metal foil to airliners.

A few metals, such as gold and platinum, can be found and mined in their pure form. But more often metals occur as part of a mineral which contains other elements. If this mixture is worth mining, it is called an ore. For example, bauxite is an ore mineral that is rich in aluminum. Ores like bauxite are mined. Then the metals are separated from them.

A steel ingot emerging from the furnace

Many metals such as steel and aluminum are used in car engines

FUELS FROM THE EARTH

Our homes, offices and factories all need energy to heat them, light them and run their machines. Much of this energy is supplied by the minerals coal, oil and natural gas. These substances formed from dead plants and animals which lived millions of years ago. They are called fossil fuels.

Fossil fuels are made up of chemical compounds that release energy when they burn. The energy may be used directly, as it is in a car engine. Or it may be used to generate electricity, which is cleaner and easier to transport.

Fossil fuels are also important raw materials. They are made of chemical compounds which are converted into a whole variety of substances, from cosmetics to plastics.

Coal, oil and gas formation

This diagram shows how fossil fuels were formed millions of years ago. At this time some parts of the Earth were covered with swamps, trees and ferns. Tiny plants and animals lived in the swamps and seas. When the forest plants died they were covered by layers of mud and sand (1). When the plants and animals in the sea died their bodies sank to the seabed (2). Here they became trapped in layers of mud which gradually formed rock. Buried deep underground, the tree and fern remains slowly turned into coal and the plants and animals in the mudrock got hot and formed oil and natural gas (3). Now we dig mines to get the coal out of the ground and drill down to extract oil and gas (4).

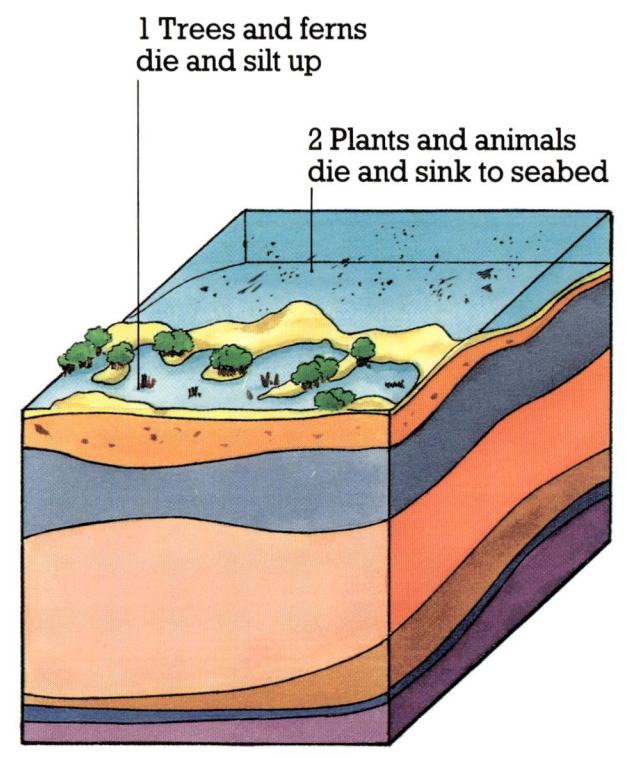

1 Trees and ferns die and silt up

2 Plants and animals die and sink to seabed

An open pit coal mine

3 Fossil fuels form from plant and animal remains buried by layers of rock

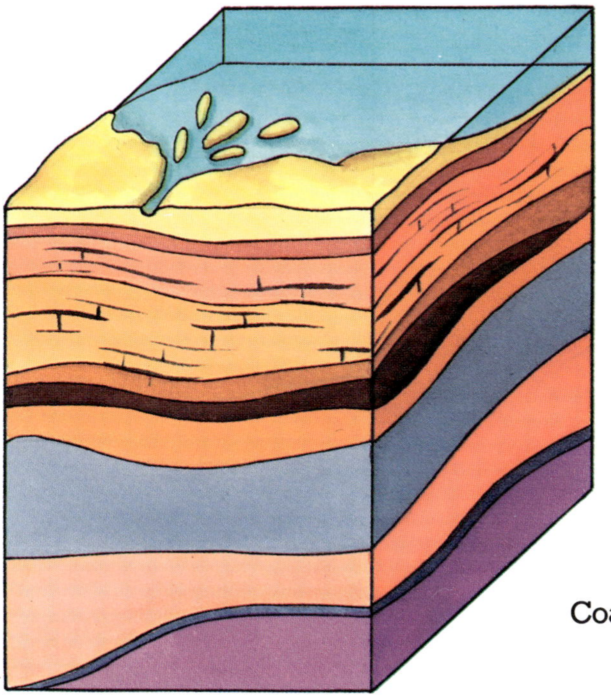

4

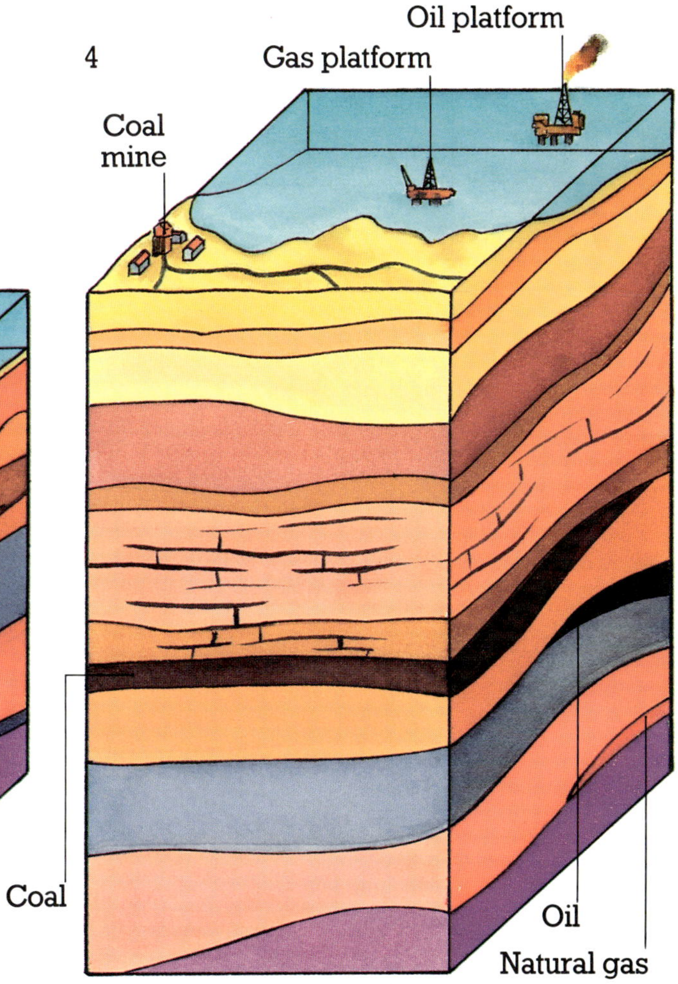

Coal mine

Gas platform

Oil platform

Coal

Oil

Natural gas

NUCLEAR FUEL

One alternative to fossil fuels is nuclear fuel. The metal uranium, the main nuclear fuel, gives out a form of energy called radioactivity. Uranium is found as an ore and has to be mined. The ore is ground into a powder and dissolved in chemicals to obtain the pure metal.

Unlike coal or oil, the energy from uranium is not released by burning. Instead specially treated uranium undergoes reactions in which its atoms split to produce vast amounts of energy. This energy is then used to generate electricity.

Uranium has become one of the world's most controversial mineral products as debates continue about the safety of nuclear power stations.

Yellow cake, one stage in the extraction of uranium

Inside a nuclear power plant – uranium must be handled with extreme caution

CERAMICS

Many rocks and minerals can be baked to make materials called ceramics. Some ceramics will be very familiar to you – bricks are ceramics, and so are most bowls, plates and mugs. Ceramics have some very useful properties. They are usually hard and they do not rot or rust. They do not let heat or electricity flow through them easily – they are good insulators.

Recently many new uses have been found for ceramics. Scientists have discovered that some ceramics, called superconductors, will conduct electricity at low temperatures without heating up or expanding. Superconductors are now used in electric circuits and engine parts.

The Space Shuttle is covered in ceramic tiles to protect it from burning up

These ceramic insulators stop energy from escaping from power lines

BRICKS AND TILES

Unless it is made of wood, your home is probably built from rocks and minerals. Perhaps it is made of bricks. Bricks make excellent building materials – they are hardly affected by the weather and they do not burn.

Bricks are made from clay, a soft sedimentary rock. Clay is found and mined in most countries in the world. It is then fired (baked) in a special oven called a kiln.

Bricks come in different colors and qualities, depending on the type of clay. Bricks can also be made from a mixture of lime and sand. These bricks are normally white or gray. Roof tiles are made in a similar way to bricks.

Making bricks

First the clay or shale (rock made from clay) is crushed. This happens at least two times. Oversize particles are screened out and put back into the crushers. When the particles are fine enough they are fed into a container and mixed with water. Wet clay is then pushed through an extruder, which molds the clay into a ribbon. Hollows may be pushed into the top of each brick before the bricks are cut and separated. The bricks are dried and fired in a kiln.

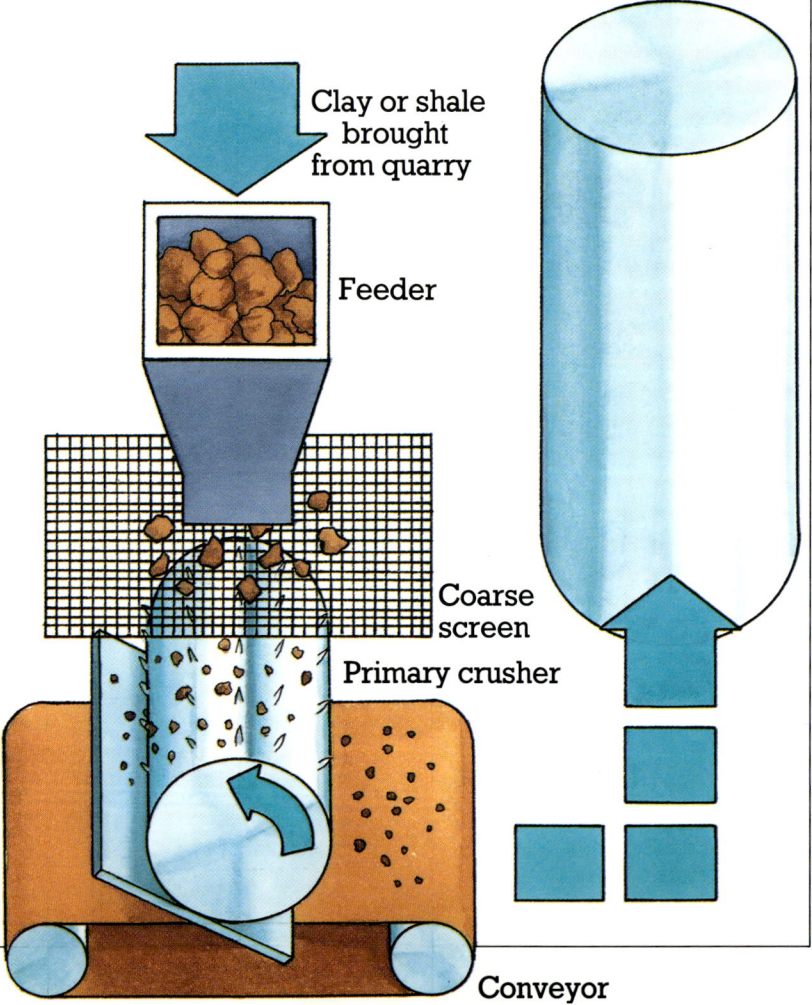

Bricks being made by hand in Tunisia

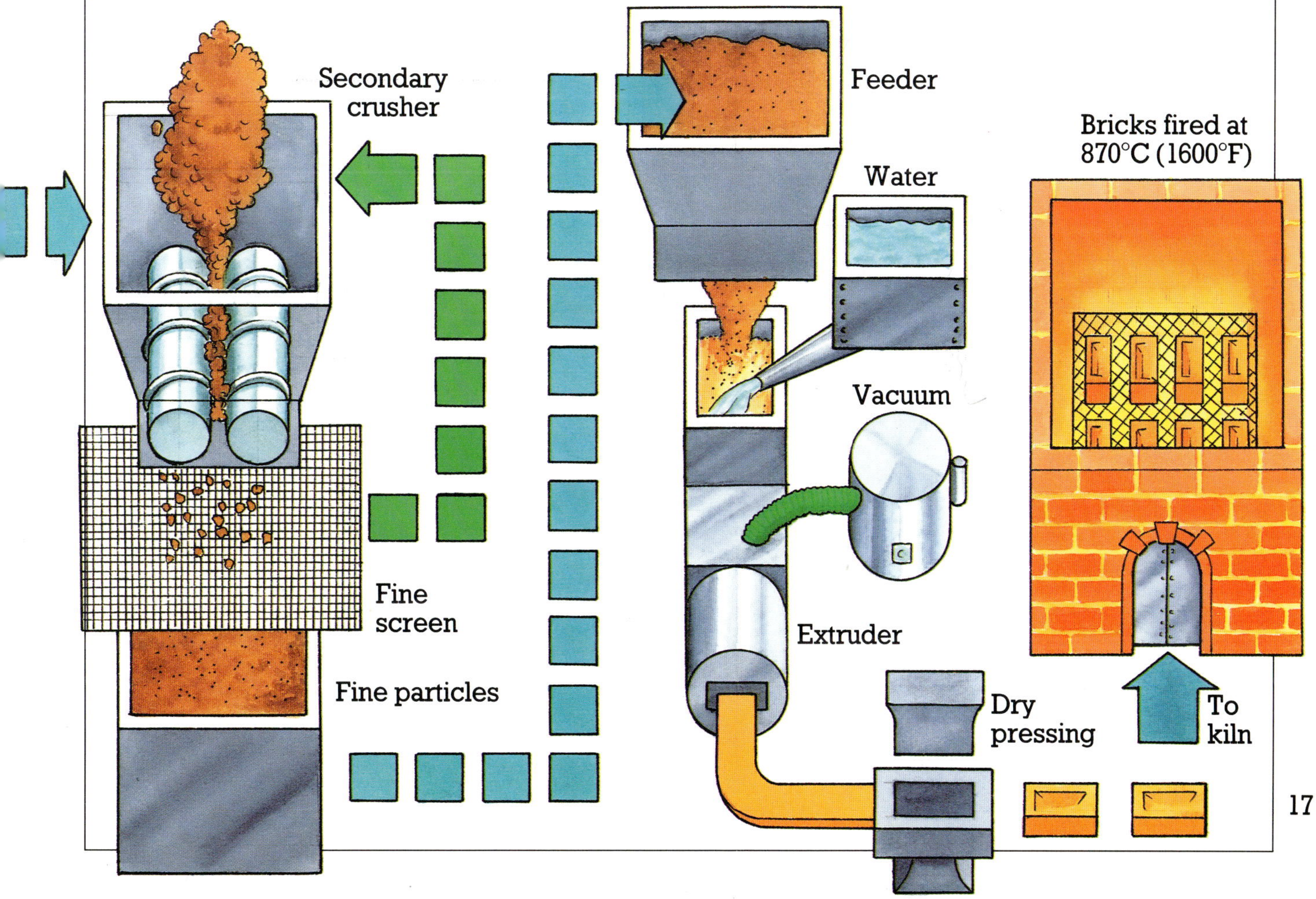

- Secondary crusher
- Fine screen
- Fine particles
- Feeder
- Water
- Vacuum
- Extruder
- Dry pressing
- To kiln
- Bricks fired at 870°C (1600°F)

CEMENT AND STONE

Some rocks – often called stones – can simply be cut into blocks for building. Sandstone, granite and limestone are all building stones. Slate is a type of clay which forms in sheets. It can be cut into flat blocks for roofs or paving stones. Marble, a rock formed from limestone, is smooth and colorful. It is used for sculpture and decoration because of its attractive appearance.

Limestone has another important use in building – it is the main constituent of cement. Cement is used to make mortar, which holds bricks together, and concrete. Concrete is our most important building material – bridges, buildings, dams and roads are all made with it.

Most modern buildings are made with concrete

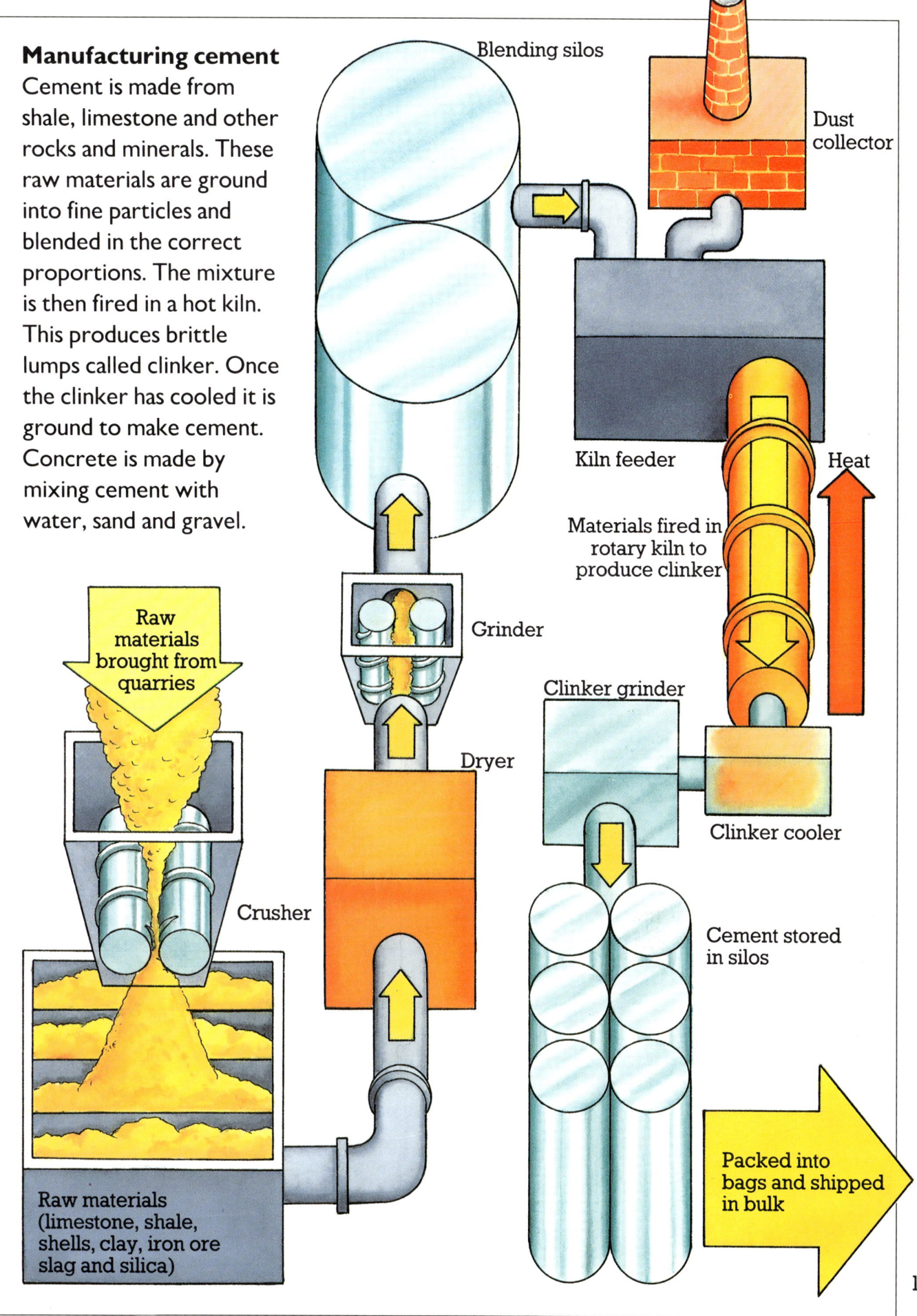

THE SILICON CHIP

Quartz, or silicon dioxide, is one of the most common minerals in the Earth's crust – sand is full of it. Quartz is the raw material used to produce silicon chips.

So what is a chip? A chip is a tiny piece of silicon smaller than your fingernail. And yet it is packed with thousands of electronic circuits which can process and store vast amounts of information. The chip is not only tiny, it is also cheap to produce. The silicon chip has changed our lives. With its help banks, libraries and supermarkets have been computerized, and irons and toasters have become programmable. New uses for the chip are being found all the time.

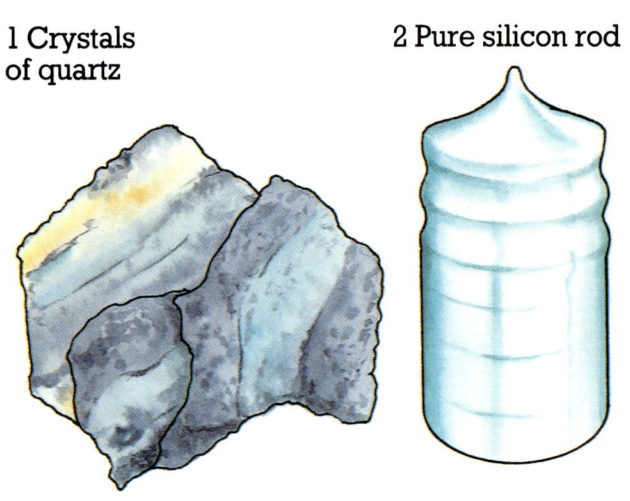
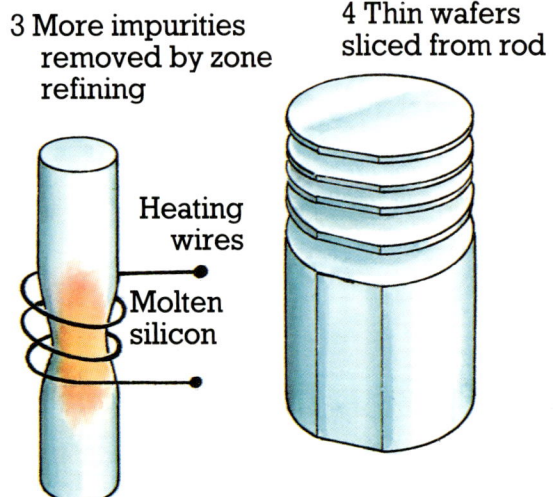

1 Crystals of quartz

2 Pure silicon rod

3 More impurities removed by zone refining

Heating wires

Molten silicon

4 Thin wafers sliced from rod

Preparing silicon for chips
Because the circuits on a chip are so small the silicon used to make it must be very pure. First silicon dioxide, found in sand and quartz rocks (1), is changed into the form of a single crystal where all the particles of silicon are arranged in orderly rows.

This is done by using a tiny crystal – called a seed crystal – to grow a rod of pure silicon (2). More impurities are pushed out by melting and cooling the rod in a process called zone refining (3). It is then sliced into thin wafers, each about 10 cm (4in) in diameter (4). One wafer will make hundreds of chips.

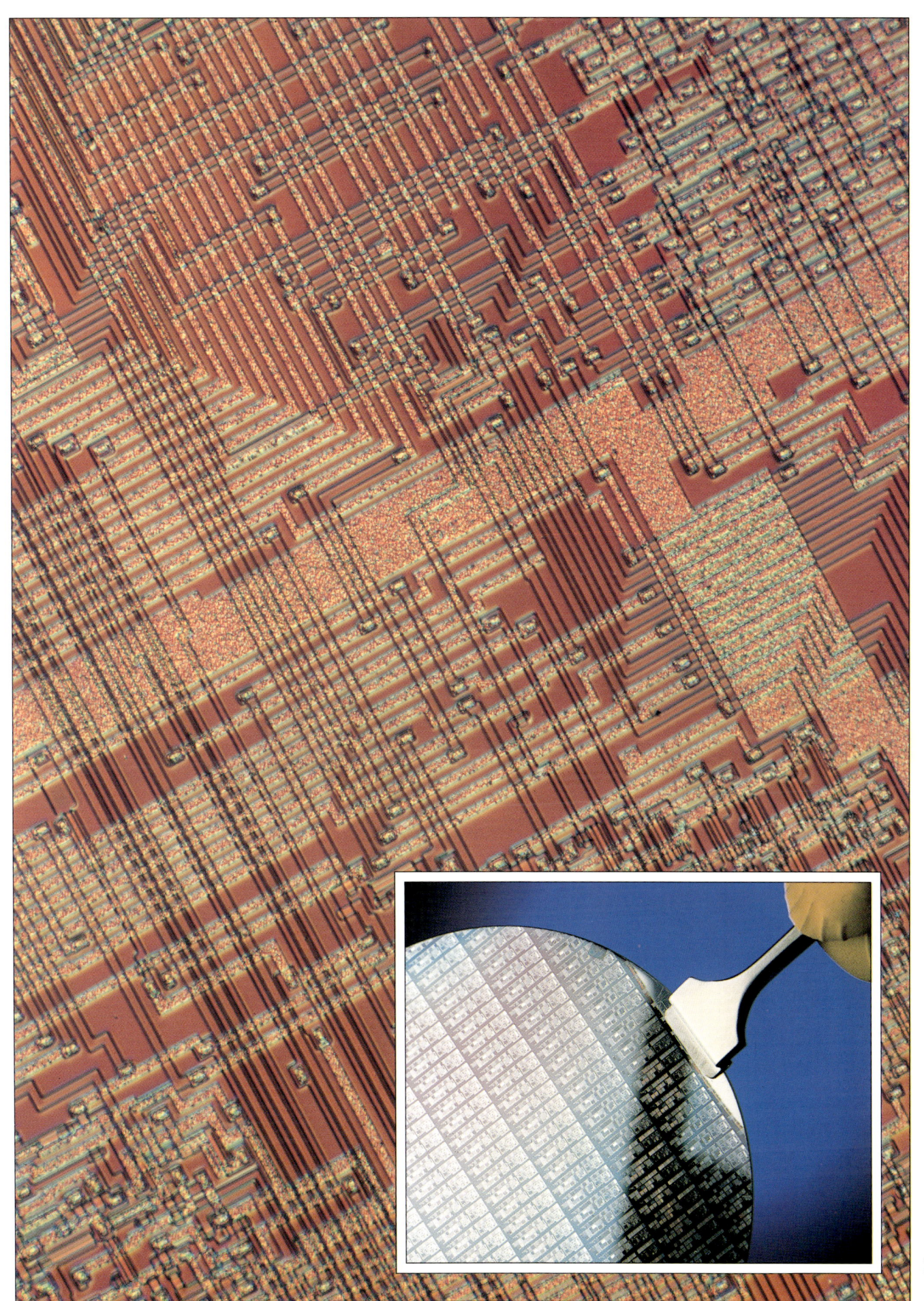
A close look at circuits on a silicon chip – the inset shows chips on a wafer

FERTILIZERS AND DRUGS

All living things, including people, need minerals to keep healthy. Humans get most of the minerals they need from food. For example, milk contains calcium needed for strong teeth and bones. Many drugs contain mineral-rich elements such as mercury and iodine. Chemicals from crude oil are used to make a whole range of drugs.

Fertilizers, which are special mixtures of minerals, are used to help plants grow. The most important minerals in fertilizers are nitrates, phosphates and potassium salts. Large quantities of fertilizers are made from these minerals. Farmers then add them to the soil.

Making fertilizers
Large quantities of fertilizers are manufactured. The diagram shows how this is done. Rock containing phosphate is crushed and mixed with phosphoric acid, nitric acid and ammonia. Water keeps the reacting chemicals cool. Potassium chloride is added and the whole mixture is stored in pools.

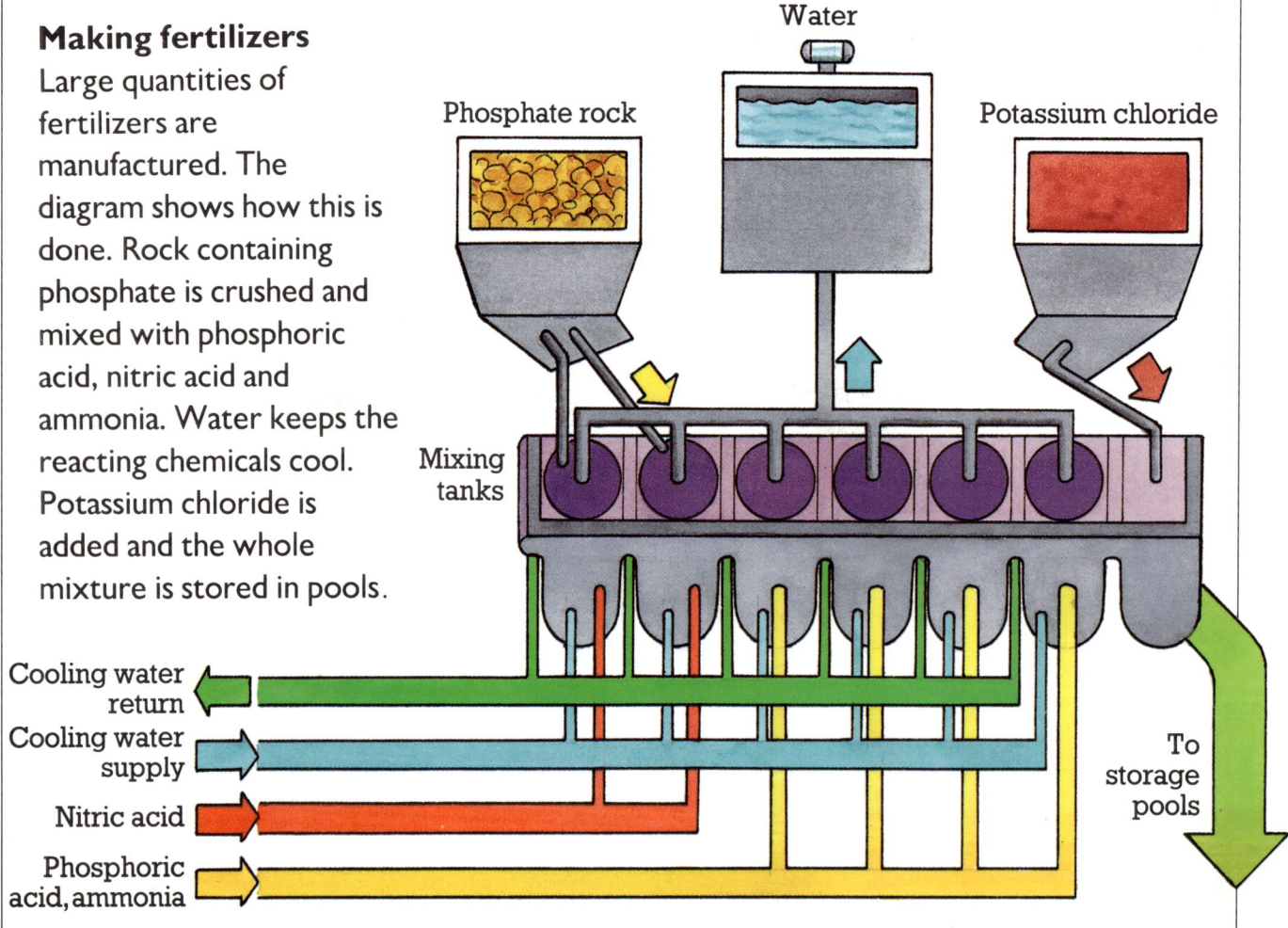

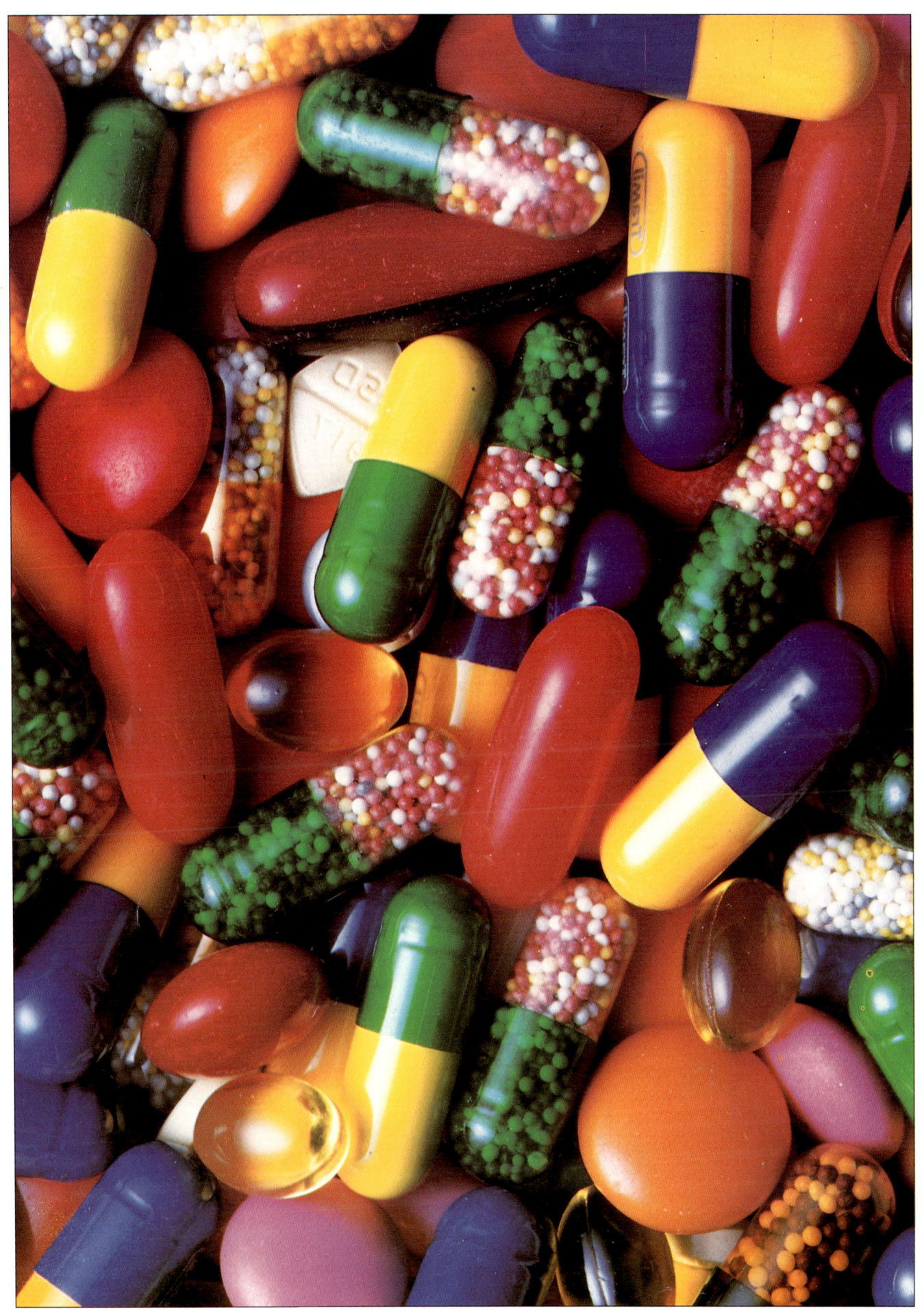
Most drugs contain minerals or are made with chemicals from oil

GEMSTONES

Some minerals form beautiful crystals. These crystals are called gems. Like other minerals gems have to be dug out of the Earth. Many diamonds come from very big, deep mines. Other gems, like opal, topaz and emerald, are mined closer to the surface. Gems are used to make jewelry, but also have important uses in industry.

Diamond is the hardest material known. It has many applications. Small or poorly colored diamonds, called industrial diamonds, are used to make saws which can cut through steel. Diamond powder and grit is also made artificially for this purpose. Quartz crystal can be made to vibrate regularly. It is used in clocks and watches.

Gems are part of the workings of this 17-jewel watch

This dentist's drill has a surface of diamond grit

STORY OF A SILICON CHIP

1. QUARTZ CRYSTAL (SILICA) IS MINED AND SENT TO THE CHIP FACTORY. 2. WHERE IT IS CHANGED INTO A SINGLE ROD OF PURE SILICON. THE ROD IS SLICED INTO THIN WAFERS, EACH ABOUT 10cm (4in) IN DIAMETER AND 0.2mm (0.0008in) THICK. (SEE PAGE 20)

7. THE WAFER IS COATED WITH SILICA AND A LIGHT-SENSITIVE MATERIAL CALLED PHOTO-RESIST. 8. THE FIRST MASK IS LAID ON THE WAFER, WHICH IS THEN EXPOSED TO ULTRA-VIOLET LIGHT, WASHED WITH ACID AND "DOPED" WITH CHEMICAL IMPURITIES. THIS LEAVES A COPY OF THE CIRCUIT PRINTED ON THE WAFER. THIS IS DONE SEVERAL TIMES UNTIL ALL THE LAYERS OF THE CIRCUIT HAVE BEEN LAID DOWN 9. 10. THE WAFERS ARE THEN CHECKED.

3. THE SILICON WAFERS ARE CUT IN A DUST-FREE ENVIRONMENT. 4. MEANWHILE THE DESIGNERS, HAVING MAPPED OUT THE CIRCUIT ON A COMPUTER, 5, PRODUCE MASKS (PATTERNS) FOR THE VARIOUS LAYERS OF THE CIRCUIT ON FILM. EACH MASK IS THE SAME SIZE AS A WAFER 6. THEN THEY REDUCE AND DUPLICATE THEM, PRODUCING HUNDREDS OF COPIES OF EACH MASK.

11. THE INDIVIDUAL CHIPS ARE CUT FROM THE WAFER, SOLDERED TO FINE GOLD WIRES, AND PUT INTO A FRAME. 12. THE FRAME IS SEALED IN A PLASTIC CASE AND THE "LEGS" ARE BENT DOWN READY TO BE INSERTED INTO A CIRCUIT BOARD — IN THIS CASE, OF A POCKET CALCULATOR 13.

FACT FILE 1

The map on the right shows where the major minerals come from. Chemical and fertilizer minerals include sulfur, rock salt, borax and phosphate rock. The largest deposits of these are in Europe, Africa and the Americas. Some 90 percent of the world's sulfur comes from Louisiana and Texas. Diamonds, the most important gemstone, are mined in Zaire, South Africa and the USSR.

More iron is produced than any other metal. Every year, 900 million tons of iron ore are mined. The main deposits are in the USSR. Bauxite, the ore of aluminum, is mined in North America, the USSR, Jamaica, Japan and Australia. Uranium ore is mined in the United States, Australia and Zaire. The largest deposits of gold, a precious metal, are in South Africa and the USSR. Large quantities are also mined in Australia, North America and central Africa.

Other industrial minerals include asbestos, china clay, mica and talc. The biggest deposits are in the United States, Europe and the USSR.

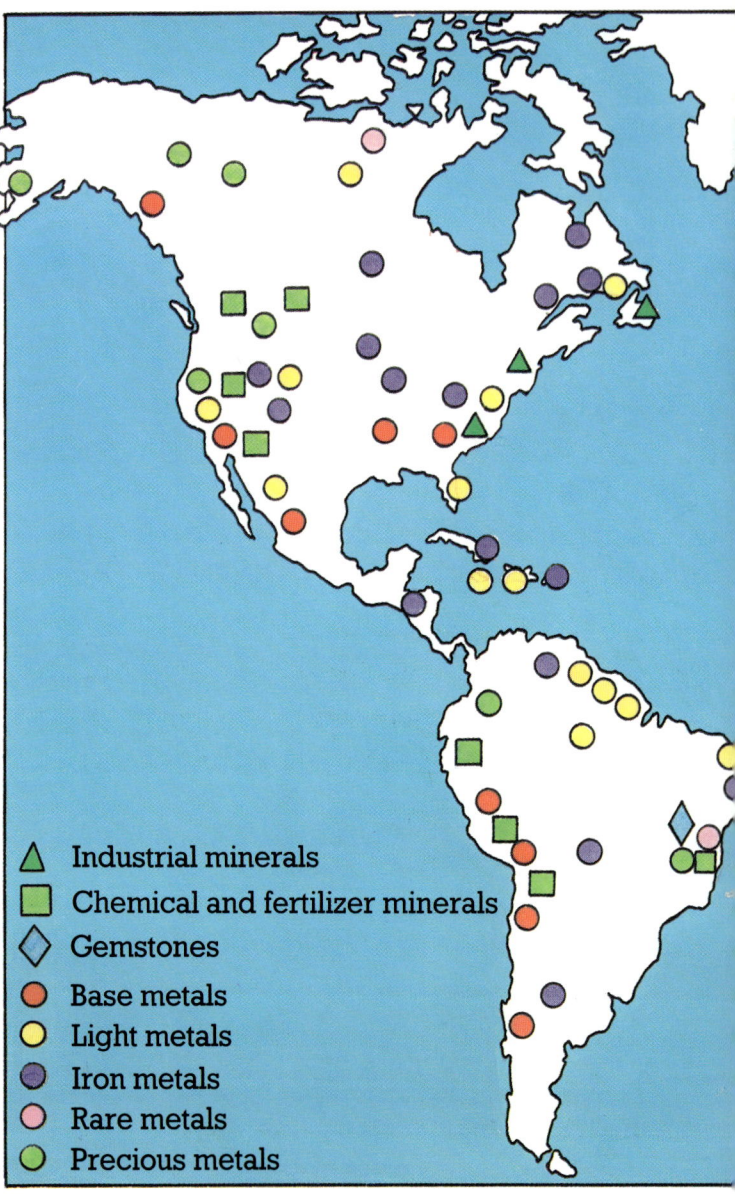

△ Industrial minerals
▢ Chemical and fertilizer minerals
◇ Gemstones
● Base metals
○ Light metals
● Iron metals
● Rare metals
● Precious metals

Fossil fuels

The map on the far right shows where the main deposits of fossil fuels have been found. More than half the known reserves of oil are in the Middle East. The USSR actually produces more oil than any other country. Some 40 percent of the world's natural gas is also found there. Every day we use over 55 million barrels of oil to supply energy needs and to manufacture chemicals such as plastics and dyes.

Coal is found on every continent, though the United States and the USSR have the largest reserves. Hard coals are a lot older than soft coals – they burn more easily and provide more energy by weight. Coal reserves will last much longer than reserves of oil and gas. So demand for coal is likely to increase in the future.

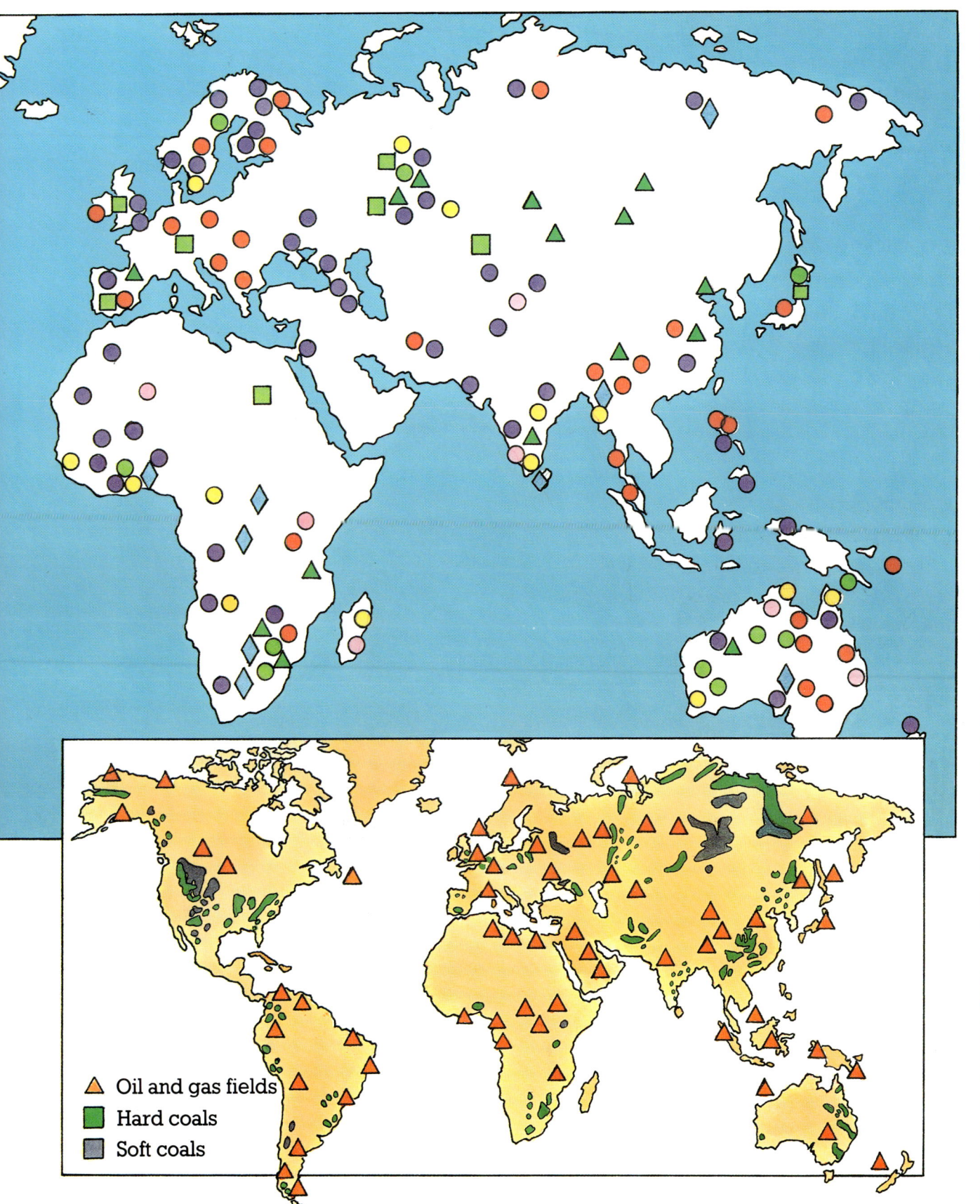

- △ Oil and gas fields
- ■ Hard coals
- ■ Soft coals

FACT FILE 2

Liquid crystal displays
Some minerals – such as those containing the metal lithium – can be used to make liquid crystals. These are half solid and half liquid. They are normally transparent, but when an electric current passes through them they turn black or green.

In a digital watch currents are passed through liquid crystals to make a display of dark numbers on a light background. The current is applied at different spots to produce different numbers.

Mineral	How it is extracted	What it is used for
HALITE (Salt)	Solution mining is used to extract deposits underground. Sea water may be evaporated.	Salt is added to food to preserve it or to enhance taste.
QUARTZ	Quartz may be mined from granite rocks or extracted from sand or gravel.	It is used in watches and to make optical instruments. It is a source of silicon for chips.
GRAPHITE	Graphite is mined from rocks such as gneiss and schist.	It is used as "lead" in pencils, as a lubricant, in paint and to make parts for electric motors.
BORAX	Borax is obtained from the beds of dry salt lakes or by evaporating sea water.	It is used in bleaches, soaps and detergents. It is also added to ceramics and fertilizers.
PHOSPHATE	Phosphate comes from phosphate rock, which is mined. Sea bird droppings also contain it.	It is used in match heads and in some medicines. But its main use is in fertilizers.

Mining rocks and minerals

The diagram below shows the main ways of mining. Deposits that are near the surface may be dug out in open pit mines (1). Some open pit mines are huge – the largest, a copper mine in the United States, covers 5.5 sq km (2 sq mi) and is 700 m (2,280 ft) deep. Deep shaft mines are also dug to reach deposits of minerals like coal or diamonds which are further underground (2). Where deposits lie in water they can be collected by a process called dredging (3).

Solution mining (4) is an alternative method for minerals such as salt. Some oil and gas is extracted from platforms at sea (5).

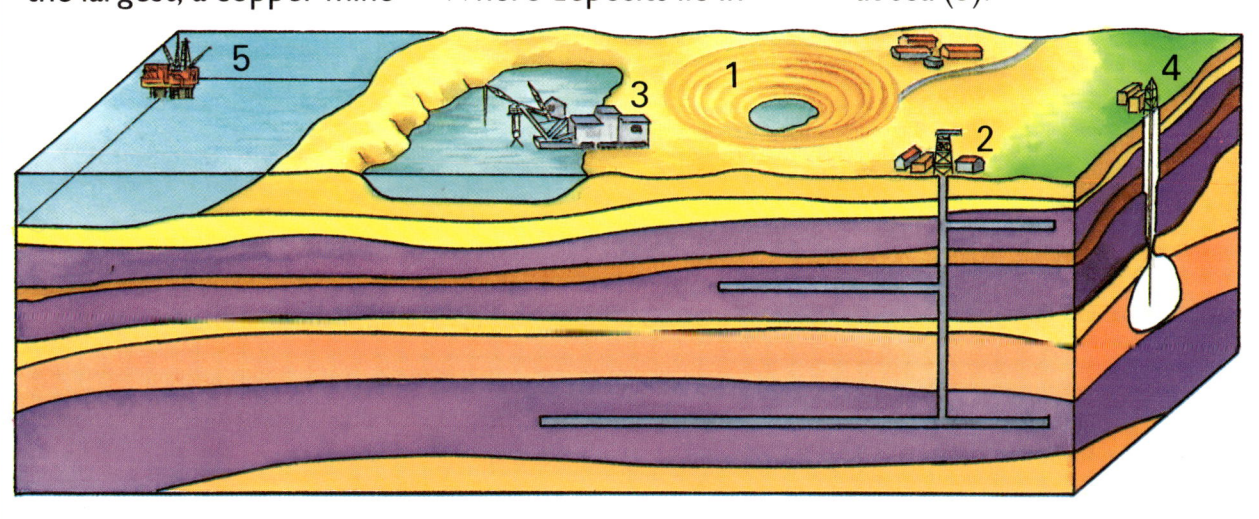

Mineral	How it is extracted	What it is used for
TITANIUM	Minerals containing it are mined and it is extracted in a protective atmosphere.	Titanium is used to make pigment for paints. It is a light, strong metal used in jet engines.
TUNGSTEN	Ores containing this metal are mined and tungsten is extracted by smelting.	It is used to make light bulb filaments, high speed drill tips and is also used in spacecraft.
GYPSUM	Gypsum is a form of calcium sulphate. It is quarried from sedimentary rocks.	Blackboard "chalk" is actually gypsum, and plaster of Paris and building plaster are made from it.
SULFUR	Sulfur is mined by being melted with hot steam. It is also extracted from some metal ores.	Its main use is the manufacture of sulfuric acid for industrial uses such as making fertilizer.
ZIRCO-NIUM	Sand containing this metal is mined and zirconium is extracted by smelting.	It is used in flash bulbs and nuclear reactor cores, and to make pumps, pipes and valves.

GLOSSARY

Concrete
A strong building material. Concrete is a mixture of sand, cement, stone and water which hardens when it dries.

Crystal
A substance made of particles which are arranged in a neat, orderly pattern.

Fertilizer
A substance containing chemicals needed for healthy plant growth.

Fossil fuel
Substances made from dead and decayed living things which produce energy when they are burned.

Kiln
A type of oven. Ceramics are baked (fired) in kilns.

Mineral
Natural chemical substances found below the Earth's surface.

Mortar
A mixture of sand, cement and water which hardens when it dries. Mortar is used to hold bricks together in building.

Ore
A mineral that is worth mining because it contains a valuable substance such as a metal.

INDEX

C
coal 10, 11, 28, 29, 31
crystals 20, 24, 26, 30

F
fossil fuels 10, 11, 28, 29

G
gas 7, 10, 11, 28, 29, 31
gems 7, 24, 25, 28, 29, 31

I
igneous rocks 6

M
magma 6, 7
metals 7, 8, 9, 12, 28, 29, 31

metamorphic rocks 7
mineral deposits 7, 28, 29, 30, 31
minerals used in:
 drugs 4, 22, 23, 30
 fertilizers 4, 22, 28, 29, 30, 31
 food 22, 30
 industry 4, 8, 9, 10, 14, 15, 20, 24, 28, 30, 31
mining 6, 7, 8, 10, 11, 12, 16, 24, 26, 28, 30, 31

O
oil 7, 10, 11, 22, 23, 28, 29, 31
ores 8, 12, 28, 31

Q
quartz 5, 20, 24, 26, 30

R
rocks:
 composition 5
 formation 6, 7
 types 5, 6, 7, 16, 18
 uses 4, 14, 16, 18, 19

S
sedimentary rocks 6, 31
silica 19, 26
stones 4, 5, 6, 18, 19

U
uranium 12, 13, 28